FORWARD/COMMENTARY

The National Institute of Standards and Technology (NIST) is a measurement standards laboratory, and a non-regulatory agency of the United States Department of Commerce. Its mission is to promote innovation and industrial competitiveness. Founded in 1901, as the National Bureau of Standards, NIST was formed with the mandate to provide standard weights and measures, and to serve as the national physical laboratory for the United States. With a world-class measurement and testing laboratory encompassing a wide range of areas of computer science, mathematics, statistics, and systems engineering, NIST's cybersecurity program supports its overall mission to promote U.S. innovation and industrial competitiveness by advancing measurement science, standards, and related technology through research and development in ways that enhance economic security and improve our quality of life.

The need for cybersecurity standards and best practices that address interoperability, usability and privacy has been shown to be critical for the nation. NIST's cybersecurity programs seek to enable greater development and application of practical, innovative security technologies and methodologies that enhance the country's ability to address current and future computer and information security challenges.

The cybersecurity publications produced by NIST cover a wide range of cybersecurity concepts that are carefully designed to work together to produce a holistic approach to cybersecurity primarily for government agencies and constitute the best practices used by industry. This holistic strategy to cybersecurity covers the gamut of security subjects from development of secure encryption standards for communication and storage of information while at rest to how best to recover from a cyber-attack.

Why buy a book you can download for free?   **We print this so you don't have to.**

Some are available only in electronic media. Some online docs are missing pages or barely legible.

We at 4th Watch Publishing are former government employees, so we know how government employees actually use the standards. When a new standard is released, an engineer prints it out, punches holes and puts it in a 3-ring binder. While this is not a big deal for a 5 or 10-page document, many NIST documents are over 100 pages and printing a large document is a time-consuming effort. So, an engineer that's paid $75 an hour is spending hours simply printing out the tools needed to do the job. That's time that could be better spent doing engineering. We publish these documents so engineers can focus on what they were hired to do – engineering. It's much more cost-effective to just order the latest version from Amazon.com

If there is a standard you would like published, let us know. Our web site is: usgovpub.com

NIST Special Publication 800-56C
Revision 1

Recommendation for Key-Derivation Methods in Key-Establishment Schemes

Elaine Barker
Lily Chen
Rich Davis

This publication is available free of charge from:
https://doi.org/10.6028/NIST.SP.800-56Cr1

COMPUTER SECURITY

National Institute of
Standards and Technology
U.S. Department of Commerce

NIST Special Publication 800-56C
Revision 1

Recommendation for Key-Derivation Methods in Key-Establishment Schemes

Elaine Barker
Lily Chen
Computer Security Division
Information Technology Laboratory

Rich Davis
National Security Agency

This publication is available free of charge from:
https://doi.org/10.6028/NIST.SP.800-56Cr1

April 2018

U.S. Department of Commerce
Wilbur L. Ross, Jr., Secretary

National Institute of Standards and Technology
Walter Copan, NIST Director and Under Secretary of Commerce for Standards and Technology

Authority

This publication has been developed by the National Institute of Standards and Technology (NIST) in accordance with its statutory responsibilities under the Federal Information Security Modernization Act (FISMA) of 2014, 44 U.S.C. § 3551 *et seq.*, Public Law (P.L.) 113-283. NIST is responsible for developing information security standards and guidelines, including minimum requirements for federal information systems, but such standards and guidelines shall not apply to national security systems without the express approval of appropriate federal officials exercising policy authority over such systems. This guideline is consistent with the requirements of the Office of Management and Budget (OMB) Circular A-130.

Nothing in this publication should be taken to contradict the standards and guidelines made mandatory and binding on federal agencies by the Secretary of Commerce under statutory authority. Nor should these guidelines be interpreted as altering or superseding the existing authorities of the Secretary of Commerce, Director of the OMB, or any other federal official. This publication may be used by nongovernmental organizations on a voluntary basis and is not subject to copyright in the United States. Attribution would, however, be appreciated by NIST.

National Institute of Standards and Technology Special Publication 800-56C Revision 1
Natl. Inst. Stand. Technol. Spec. Publ. 800-56C Rev. 1, 37 pages (April 2018)
CODEN: NSPUE2

This publication is available free of charge from:
https://doi.org/10.6028/NIST.SP.800-56Cr1

Certain commercial entities, equipment, or materials may be identified in this document in order to describe an experimental procedure or concept adequately. Such identification is not intended to imply recommendation or endorsement by NIST, nor is it intended to imply that the entities, materials, or equipment are necessarily the best available for the purpose.

There may be references in this publication to other publications currently under development by NIST in accordance with its assigned statutory responsibilities. The information in this publication, including concepts and methodologies, may be used by federal agencies even before the completion of such companion publications. Thus, until each publication is completed, current requirements, guidelines, and procedures, where they exist, remain operative. For planning and transition purposes, federal agencies may wish to closely follow the development of these new publications by NIST.

Organizations are encouraged to review all draft publications during public comment periods and provide feedback to NIST. Many NIST cybersecurity publications, other than the ones noted above, are available at https://csrc.nist.gov/publications.

Comments on this publication may be submitted to:

National Institute of Standards and Technology
Attn: Computer Security Division, Information Technology Laboratory
100 Bureau Drive (Mail Stop 8930) Gaithersburg, MD 20899-8930
Email: 800-56C_Comments@nist.gov

All comments are subject to release under the Freedom of Information Act (FOIA).

Reports on Computer Systems Technology

The Information Technology Laboratory (ITL) at the National Institute of Standards and Technology (NIST) promotes the U.S. economy and public welfare by providing technical leadership for the Nation's measurement and standards infrastructure. ITL develops tests, test methods, reference data, proof of concept implementations, and technical analyses to advance the development and productive use of information technology. ITL's responsibilities include the development of management, administrative, technical, and physical standards and guidelines for the cost-effective security and privacy of other than national security-related information in federal information systems. The Special Publication 800-series reports on ITL's research, guidelines, and outreach efforts in information system security, and its collaborative activities with industry, government, and academic organizations.

Abstract

This Recommendation specifies techniques for the derivation of keying material from a shared secret established during a key-establishment scheme defined in NIST Special Publications 800-56A or 800-56B.

Keywords

Expansion, extraction, extraction-then-expansion, hash function, key derivation, key establishment, message authentication code.

Acknowledgements

The authors gratefully acknowledge the contributions on this and previous versions of this document by their NIST colleagues (Quynh Dang, Sharon Keller, John Kelsey, Allen Roginsky, Meltem Sonmez Turan, Apostol Vassilev, and Tim Polk) and by Miles Smid, formerly of Orion Security Solutions.

The authors also gratefully appreciate the thoughtful and instructive comments received during the public comment periods, which helped to improve the quality of this publication.

Conformance Testing

Conformance testing for implementations of the functions that are specified in this publication will be conducted within the framework of the Cryptographic Algorithm Validation Program (CAVP) and the Cryptographic Module Validation Program (CMVP). The requirements on these implementations are indicated by the word "shall." Some of these requirements may be out-of-scope for CAVP or CMVP validation testing, and thus are the responsibility of entities using, implementing, installing, or configuring applications that incorporate this Recommendation.

Table of Contents

List of Figures

List of Tables

1   Introduction

During the execution of a public-key-based key-establishment scheme specified in either of the National Institute of Standards and Technology (NIST) Special Publications [SP 800-56A][1] or [SP 800-56B][2], a key-derivation method may be required to obtain secret cryptographic keying material. This Recommendation specifies the key-derivation methods that can be used, as needed, in those key-establishment schemes. The keying material derived using these methods **shall** be computed in its entirety before outputting any portion of it, and **shall** only be used as secret keying material – such as a symmetric key used for data encryption or message integrity, a secret initialization vector, or, perhaps, a key-derivation key that will be used to generate additional keying material (possibly using a different derivation process – see [SP 800-108][3]). The derived keying material **shall not** be used as a key stream for a stream cipher.

---

[1] SP 800-56A, *Recommendation for Pair-Wise Key-Establishment Schemes Using Discrete Logarithm Cryptography.*

[2] SP 800-56B, *Recommendation for Pair-Wise Key-Establishment Schemes Using Integer Factorization Cryptography.*

[3] SP 800-108, *Recommendation for Key Derivation Using Pseudorandom Functions (Revised).*

2 Scope and Purpose

This Recommendation specifies two categories of key-derivation methods that can be employed, as required, as part of a key-establishment scheme specified in [SP 800-56A] or [SP 800-56B].

The first category consists of a family of one-step key-derivation functions, which derive keying material of a desired length from a shared secret generated during the execution of a key-establishment scheme (and possibly other information as well).

The second category consists of an extraction-then-expansion key-derivation procedure, which involves two steps:

1) Randomness extraction, to obtain a single cryptographic key-derivation key from a shared secret generated during the execution of a key-establishment scheme, and

2) Key expansion, to derive keying material of the desired length from that key-derivation key and other information. Since NIST's [SP 800-108] specifies several families of key-derivation functions that are **approved** for deriving additional keying material from a given cryptographic key-derivation key, those functions are employed in the second (key-expansion) step of these two-step procedures.

In addition to the key-derivation methods whose specifications are provided in this document, [SP 800-135][4] describes several variants (of both the one-step and two-step methods) that are **approved** for specific applications.

---

[4] SP 800-135 Rev. 1, *Recommendation for Existing Application-Specific Key Derivation Functions.*

3　Definitions, Symbols and Abbreviations

3.1　Definitions

Algorithm	A clearly specified mathematical process for computation; a set of rules that, if followed, will give a prescribed result.
Approved	An algorithm or technique that is either 1) specified in a Federal Information Processing Standard (FIPS) or NIST Recommendation, 2) adopted in a FIPS or NIST Recommendation or 3) specified in a list of NIST-approved security functions.
Big-endian	The property of a byte string having its bytes positioned in order of decreasing significance. In particular, the leftmost (first) byte is the most significant (containing the most significant eight bits of the corresponding bit string) and the rightmost (last) byte is the least significant (containing the least significant eight bits of the corresponding bit string). For the purposes of this Recommendation, it is assumed that the bits within each byte of a big-endian byte string are also positioned in order of decreasing significance (beginning with the most significant bit in the leftmost position and ending with the least significant bit in the rightmost position).
Bit length	The number of bits in a bit string. E.g., the bit length of the string 0110010101000011 is sixteen bits. The bit length of the empty (i.e., null) string is zero.
Bit string	An ordered sequence of bits (represented as 0's and 1's). Unless otherwise stated in this document, bit strings are depicted as beginning with their most significant bit (shown in the leftmost position) and ending with their least significant bit (shown in the rightmost position). E.g., the most significant (leftmost) bit of 0101 is 0, and its least significant (rightmost) bit is 1. If interpreted as the 4-bit binary representation of an unsigned integer, 0101 corresponds to five.
Byte	A bit string consisting of eight bits.
Byte length	The number of consecutive (non-overlapping) bytes in a byte string. For example, $0110010101000011 = 01100101 \,\|\, 01000011$ is two bytes long. The byte length of the empty string is zero.
Byte string	An ordered sequence of bytes, beginning with the most significant (leftmost) byte and ending with the least significant (rightmost)

	byte. Any bit string whose bit length is a multiple of eight can be viewed as the concatenation of an ordered sequence of bytes, i.e., a byte string. E.g., the bit string 0110010101000011 can be viewed as a byte string, since it is the concatenation of two bytes: 01100101 followed by 01000011.
Concatenation	As used in this Recommendation, the concatenation, $X \parallel Y$, of bit string X followed by bit string Y is the ordered sequence of bits formed by appending Y to X in such a way that the leftmost (i.e., initial) bit of Y follows the rightmost (i.e., final) bit of X.
Cryptographic key (Key)	A parameter used with a cryptographic algorithm that determines its operation.
Estimated maximum security strength	An estimate of the largest security strength that can be attained by a cryptographic mechanism, given the explicit and implicit assumptions that are made regarding its implementation and supporting infrastructure (e.g., the algorithms employed, the selection of associated primitives and/or auxiliary functions, the choices for various parameters, the methods of generation and/or protection for any required keys, etc.). The estimated maximum security strengths of various **approved** cryptographic mechanisms are provided in [SP 800-57].
Hash function	A function that maps a bit string of arbitrary length to a fixed-length bit string. **Approved** hash functions are designed to satisfy the following properties: 1. (One-way) It is computationally infeasible to find any input that maps to any pre-specified output, and 2. (Collision resistant) It is computationally infeasible to find any two distinct inputs that map to the same output. **Approved** hash functions are specified in [FIPS 180][5] and [FIPS 202][6].
Key-derivation function	As used in this Recommendation, either a one-step key-derivation method, or a key-derivation function based on a pseudorandom function as specified in [SP 800-108].

---

[5] FIPS 180, *Secure Hash Standard (SHS).*
[6] FIPS 202, *SHA-3 Standard: Permutation-Based Hash and Extendable-Output Functions.*

Key-derivation method	As used in this Recommendation, a process that derives secret keying material from a shared secret. This Recommendation specifies both one-step and two-step key-derivation methods.
Key-derivation procedure	As used in this Recommendation, a two-step key-derivation method consisting of randomness extraction followed by key expansion.
Key-derivation key	As used in this Recommendation, a key that is used during the key-expansion step of a key-derivation procedure to derive the secret output keying material. This key-derivation key is obtained from a shared secret during the randomness-extraction step.
Key establishment	A procedure that results in secret keying material that is shared among different parties.
Key expansion	The second step in the key-derivation procedure specified in this Recommendation, in which a key-derivation key is used to derive secret keying material having the desired length.
Keying material	Data that is represented as a binary string such that any non-overlapping segments of the string with the required lengths can be used as secret keys, secret initialization vectors and other secret parameters.
Message Authentication Code (MAC) algorithm	A family of cryptographic functions that is parameterized by a symmetric key. Each of the functions can act on input data (called a "message") of variable length to produce an output value of a specified length. The output value is called the MAC of the input message. $MAC(k, x, \ldots)$ is used to denote the MAC of message x computed using the key k (and any additional algorithm-specific parameters). An **approved** MAC algorithm is expected to satisfy the following property (for each supported security strength): Without knowledge of the key k, it must be computationally infeasible to predict the (as-yet-unseen) value of $MAC(k, x, \ldots)$ with a probability of success that is a significant improvement over simply guessing either the MAC value or k, even if one has already seen the results of using that same key to compute $MAC(k, x_j, \ldots)$ for (a bounded number of) other messages $x_j \neq x$. A MAC algorithm can be employed to provide authentication of the origin of data and/or to provide data-integrity protection. In this Recommendation, **approved** MAC algorithms are used to determine families of pseudorandom functions (indexed by the choice of key) that may be employed during key derivation.

Nonce	A varying value that has at most a negligible chance of repeating – for example, a random value that is generated anew for each use, a timestamp, a sequence number, or some combination of these.
Pseudorandom function family (PRF)	An indexed family of (efficiently computable) functions, each defined for the same particular pair of input and output spaces. (For the purposes of this Recommendation, one may assume that both the index set and the output space are finite.) The indexed functions are pseudorandom in the following sense: If a function from the family is selected by choosing an index value uniformly at random, and one's knowledge of the selected function is limited to the output values corresponding to a feasible number of (adaptively) chosen input values, then the selected function is computationally indistinguishable from a function whose outputs were fixed uniformly at random.
Randomness extraction	The first step in the two-step key-derivation procedure specified in this Recommendation; during this step, a key-derivation key is produced from a shared secret.
Salt	As used in this Recommendation, a byte string (which may be secret or non-secret) that is used as a MAC key by either 1) a MAC-based auxiliary function H employed in one-step key derivation, or, 2) a MAC employed in the randomness-extraction step during two-step key derivation.
Security strength	A number characterizing the amount of work that is expected to suffice to "defeat" an implemented cryptographic mechanism (e.g., by compromising its functionality and/or circumventing the protection that its use was intended to facilitate). In this Recommendation, security strength is measured in bits. If the security strength of a particular implementation of a cryptographic mechanism is s bits, it is expected that the equivalent of (roughly) 2^s basic operations of some sort will be sufficient to defeat it in some way.
Shared secret	The secret byte string that is computed/generated during the execution of an **approved** key-establishment scheme and used as input to a key-derivation method as part of that transaction.
Shall	A requirement that needs to be fulfilled to claim conformance to this Recommendation. Note that **shall** may be coupled with **not** to become **shall not**.

Support (a security strength)	A security strength of s bits is said to be supported by a particular choice of algorithm, primitive, auxiliary function, parameters (etc.) for use in the implementation of a cryptographic mechanism if that choice will not prevent the resulting implementation from attaining a security strength of at least s bits. In this Recommendation, it is assumed that implementation choices are intended to support a security strength of 112 bits or more (see [SP 800-57][7] and [SP 800-131A][8]).
Symmetric key	A single cryptographic key that is used with a symmetric-key algorithm. Also called a secret key. A symmetric-key algorithm is a cryptographic algorithm that uses the same secret key for an operation and its complement (e.g., encryption and decryption).
Targeted security strength	The security strength that is intended to be supported by one or more implementation-related choices (such as algorithms, primitives, auxiliary functions, parameter sizes and/or actual parameters) for the purpose of implementing a cryptographic mechanism.

3.2   Symbols and Abbreviations

0x	A marker used to indicate that the following symbols are to be interpreted as a bit string written in hexadecimal notation (using the symbols 0, 1, …, 9, and A, B, …, F to denote 4-bit binary representations of the integers zero through nine and ten through fifteen, respectively). A byte can be represented by a hexadecimal string of length two; the leftmost hexadecimal symbol corresponds to the most significant four bits of the byte, and the rightmost hexadecimal symbol corresponds to the least significant four bits of the byte. For example, 0x9D represents the bit string 10011101 (assuming that the bits are positioned in order of decreasing significance).
AES	Advanced Encryption Standard (the block cipher specified in [FIPS 197][9]).
AES-N	The variant of the AES block cipher that requires an N-bit encryption/decryption key; the three variants specified in

---

[7] SP 800-57 Rev. 4, *Recommendation for Key Management Part1: General.*

[8] SP 800-131A, *Transitions: Recommendation for Transitioning the Use of Cryptographic Algorithms and Key Lengths.*

[9] FIPS 197, *Advanced Encryption Standard.*

(N = 128, 192, or 256)	[FIPS 197] are AES-128, AES-192, and AES-256.
AES-CMAC	The Cipher-based Message Authentication Code (CMAC) mode of operation for the AES block cipher, as specified in [SP 800-38B][10].
AES-N-CMAC(k, x) (N = 128, 192, or 256)	An implementation of AES-CMAC based on the AES-N variant of the AES block cipher (for N = 128, 192, or 256); its output is a 128-bit MAC computed over the "message" x using the key k.
counter	An unsigned integer, represented as a big-endian four-byte string, that is employed by the one-step key-derivation method specified in Section 4.1.
Context	A bit string of context-specific data; a subcomponent of the *FixedInfo* that is included as part of the input to the two-step key-derivation method specified in Section 5.1.
default_salt	A default value assigned to *salt* (if necessary) to implement an auxiliary function H selected according to Option 2 or 3 in the one-step key-derivation method specified in Section 4.1.
DerivedKeyingMaterial	Keying material that is derived from a shared secret Z (and other data) through the use of a key-derivation method.
ECC	Elliptic curve cryptography.
$enc_8(x)$	A one-byte encoding of an integer x, where $0 \leq x \leq 255$, with bit 0 being the low-order (least significant) bit and bit 7 being the high-order (most significant) bit.
FFC	Finite field cryptography.
FixedInfo	A bit string of context-specific data whose value does not change during the execution of a key-derivation method specified in this Recommendation.
H	The auxiliary function used to produce blocks of keying material during the execution of the one-step key-derivation method specified in Section 4.1.

---

[10] SP 800-38B, *Recommendation for Block Cipher Modes of Operation: the CMAC Mode for Authentication*.

hash	A hash function. **Approved** choices for *hash* are specified in [FIPS 180] and [FIPS 202].
HMAC	Keyed-hash Message Authentication Code, as specified in [FIPS 198][11].
HMAC-*hash*(k, x)	An implementation of HMAC using the hash function, *hash*; its output is a MAC computed over "message" x using the key k.
H_outputBits	A positive integer that indicates the length (in bits) of the output of either 1) the auxiliary function H used in the one-step key-derivation method specified in Section 4.1, or, 2) an auxiliary HMAC algorithm used in the two-step key-derivation method specified in Section 5.1.
IFC	Integer factorization cryptography.
IV	Initialization vector; as used in this Recommendation, it is a bit string used as an initial value during the execution of an **approved** PRF-based KDF operating in Feedback Mode, as specified in [SP 800-108].
KDF	Key-derivation function.
K_{DK}	The key-derivation key resulting from the randomness-extraction step and then used in the key-expansion step during the execution of the key-derivation procedure specified in Section 5.1.
KDM	Key-derivation method.
KMAC	Keccak Message Authentication Code, as specified in [SP 800-185][12].
KMAC#(k, x, l, S)	A variant of KMAC (either KMAC128 or KMAC256, as specified in [SP 800-185]); its output is an l-bit MAC computed over the "message" x using the key k and "customization string" S.
L	A positive integer specifying the desired length (in bits) of

---

[11] FIPS 198, *The Keyed-Hash Message Authentication Code (HMAC)*.

[12] SP 800-185, SHA-3 Derived Functions: *cSHAKE, KMAC, TupleHash and ParallelHash*.

	the derived keying material.
$[L]_2$	An agreed-upon encoding of the integer L as a bit string.
MAC	Message Authentication Code.
MAC($k, x, \ldots$)	An instance of a MAC algorithm computed over the "message" x using the key k (and any additional algorithm-specific parameters).
max_H_inputBits	The maximum length (in bits) for strings used as input to the auxiliary function H employed by the one-step key-derivation method specified in Section 4.1.
OtherInput	A collective term for any and all additional data (other than the shared secret itself) used as input to a key-derivation method specified in this Recommendation.
PRF	Pseudorandom function (family).
s	Security strength (in bits).
SHA	Secure Hash Algorithm, as specified in [FIPS 180] (i.e., SHA-1, SHA-224, SHA-512/224, SHA-256, SHA-512/256, SHA-384, or SHA-512) or [FIPS 202] (i.e., SHA3-224, SHA3-256, SHA3-384, or SHA3-512).
Z	Shared secret (determined according to the specifications in either [SP 800-56A] or [SP 800-56B]).

4   One-Step Key Derivation

This section specifies a family of **approved** key-derivation functions (KDFs) that are executed in a single step; a two-step procedure is specified in Section 5. The input to each specified KDF includes the shared secret generated during the execution of a key-establishment scheme specified in [SP 800-56A] or [SP 800-56B], an indication of the desired bit length of the keying material to be output, and, perhaps, other information (as determined by the particular implementation of the key-establishment scheme and/or key-derivation function).

Implementations of these one-step KDFs depend upon the choice of an auxiliary function H, which can be either 1) an **approved** hash function, denoted as *hash*, as defined in [FIPS 180] or [FIPS 202]; 2) HMAC with an **approved** hash function, *hash*, denoted as HMAC-*hash*, and defined in [FIPS 198]; or 3) a KMAC variant, as defined in [SP 800-185]. Tables 1, 2, and 3 in Section 4.2 describe the possibilities for H, and also include any restrictions on the associated implementation-dependent parameters. H **shall** be chosen in accordance with the selection requirements specified in Section 7.

When an **approved** MAC algorithm (HMAC or KMAC) is used to define the auxiliary function H, it is permitted to use a known *salt* value as the MAC key. In such cases, it is assumed that the MAC algorithm will satisfy the following property (for each of its supported security strengths):

> Given knowledge of the key k, and (perhaps) partial knowledge of a message x that includes an unknown substring z, it must be computationally infeasible to predict the (as-yet-unseen) value of MAC(k, x, …) with a probability of success that is a significant improvement over simply guessing either the MAC value or the value of z, even if one has already seen the values of MAC(k_j, x_j, …) for a feasible number of other (k_j, x_j) pairs, where each key k_j is known and each (partially known) message x_j includes the same unknown substring z, provided that none of the (k_j, x_j) pairs is identical to (k, x).

This property is consistent with the use of the MAC algorithm as the specification of a family of pseudorandom functions defined on the appropriate message space and indexed by the choice of MAC key. Under Option 2 and Option 3 of the KDF specification below, the auxiliary function H is a particular selection from such a family.

4.1   Specification of Key-Derivation Functions

A family of one-step key-derivation functions is specified as follows:

Function call: KDM(Z, *OtherInput*).

Options for the Auxiliary Function H:

Option 1:   H(x) = *hash*(x), where *hash* is an **approved** hash function meeting the selection requirements specified in Section 7, and the input, x, is a bit string.

Option 2:   H(x) = HMAC-*hash*(*salt*, x), where HMAC-*hash* is an implementation of the HMAC algorithm (as defined in [FIPS 198]) employing an **approved** hash function, *hash*, that meets the selection requirements specified in Section 7. An implementation-dependent byte string, *salt*, whose (non-null) value may be optionally provided in *OtherInput*, serves as the HMAC key, and *x* (the input to H) is a bit string that serves as the HMAC "message" – as specified in [FIPS 198].

Option 3:   H(*x*) = KMAC#(*salt*, *x*, *H_outputBits*, *S*), where KMAC# is a particular implementation of either KMAC128 or KMAC256 (as defined in [SP 800-185]) that meets the selection requirements specified in Section 7. An implementation-dependent byte string, *salt*, whose (non-null) value may be optionally provided in *OtherInput*, serves as the KMAC# key, and *x* (the input to H) is a bit string that serves as the KMAC# "message" – as specified in [SP 800-185]. The parameter *H_outputBits* determines the bit length chosen for the output of the KMAC variant employed. The "customization string" *S* **shall** be the byte string 01001011 || 01000100 || 01000110, which represents the sequence of characters "K", "D", and "F" in 8-bit ASCII. (This three-byte string is denoted by "KDF" in this document.)

Implementation-Dependent Parameters:

1. *H_outputBits* – a positive integer that indicates the length (in bits) of the output of the auxiliary function, H, that is used to derive blocks of secret keying material. If Option 1 or Option 2 is chosen, then *H_outputBits* corresponds to the bit-length of the output block of the particular hash function used in the implementation of H; therefore, *H_outputBits* is in the set {160, 224, 256, 384, 512}, with the precise value determined by the choice for the hash function, *hash* (see Section 4.2 for details). If Option 3 is chosen, then *H_outputBits* **shall** either be set equal to the length (in bits) of the secret keying material to be derived (see input *L* below) or selected from the set {160, 224, 256, 384, 512}.

2. *max_H_inputBits* – a positive integer that indicates the maximum permitted length (in bits) of the bit string, *x*, that is used as input to the auxiliary function, H. If Option 1 or Option 2 is chosen for the implementation of H, then an upper bound on *max_H_inputBits* may be determined by the choice of the hash function, *hash* (see Section 4.2 for details); *max_H_inputBits* values smaller than a specification-imposed upper bound may be dictated by the particular use case. If the hash function, *hash*, is specified in [FIPS 202], or if Option 3 is chosen for the implementation of H, then there is no specification-imposed upper bound on *max_H_inputBits*; the value assigned to *max_H_inputBits* may be determined by the needs of the relying applications/parties.

3. *default_salt* – a non-null (secret or non-secret) byte string that is needed only if either Option 2 (HMAC-*hash*) or Option 3 (KMAC#) is chosen for the implementation of the auxiliary function H. This byte string is used as the value of *salt* if a (non-null) value is <u>not</u> included in *OtherInput* (see below).

   If H(*x*) = HMAC-*hash*(*salt*, *x*), then, in the absence of an agreed-upon alternative, the *default_salt* **shall** be an all-zero byte string whose bit length equals that specified as the bit length of an input block for the hash function, *hash*. (Input-block lengths for the **approved** hash functions that can be employed to implement HMAC-*hash* are listed in Table 1 of Section 4.2.)

If H(x) = KMAC128(*salt*, x, *H_outputBits*, "KDF"), then, in the absence of an agreed-upon alternative, the *default_salt* **shall** be an all-zero string of 164 bytes (i.e., an all-zero string of 1312 bits).

If H(x) = KMAC256(*salt*, x, *H_outputBits*, "KDF"), then, in the absence of an agreed-upon alternative, the *default_salt* **shall** be an all-zero string of 132 bytes (i.e., an all-zero string of 1056 bits).

Input:

1. Z – a byte string that represents the shared secret.

2. *OtherInput*, which includes:

   a. {*salt*} – a non-null (secret or non-secret) byte string that can be (optionally) provided if either Option 2 (HMAC-*hash*) or Option 3 (KMAC#) is chosen for the implementation of the auxiliary function H, since those options require a *salt* value that is used as a MAC key.

   The *salt* included in *OtherInput* could be, for example, a value computed from nonces exchanged as part of a key-establishment protocol that employs one or more of the key-agreement schemes specified in [SP 800-56A] or [SP 800-56B], a value already shared by the protocol participants, or a value that is pre-determined by the protocol. The possibilities for the length of *salt* are determined as follows:

   (1) The HMAC-*hash* algorithm as defined in [FIPS 198] can accommodate MAC keys of any bit length permitted for input to the hash function, *hash*. Therefore, when Option 2 is chosen, the length of the byte string *salt* can be as large as allowed for any string used as input to *hash*. However, if the bit length of *salt* is greater than the bit length specified for a single input block for the hash function, *hash*, then the value of *salt* is replaced by *hash*(*salt*) as part of the HMAC computation. See Table 2 for details.

   (2) The KMAC128 and KMAC256 algorithms specified in [SP 800-185] can accommodate MAC keys of any length up to ($2^{2040} - 1$) bits. Therefore, when Option 3 is chosen, *salt* can be a byte string of any agreed-upon length that does not exceed ($2^{2037} - 1$ bytes) (i.e., $2^{2040} - 8$ bits). The input *salt* value will be (re)formatted (using a byte-padding function) during the execution of the KMAC algorithm to obtain a string whose length is a multiple of either 168 bytes (for KMAC128) or 136 bytes (for KMAC256). See Table 3 for details.

   If a *salt* value required by H is omitted from *OtherInput* (or if a required *salt* value included in *OtherInput* is the null string), then the value of *default_salt* **shall** be used as the value of *salt* when H is executed.

   b. L – a positive integer that indicates the length (in bits) of the secret keying material to be derived; L **shall not** exceed *H_outputBits* $\times (2^{32} - 1)$.

   (L = *keydatalen* in the notation of previous versions of [SP 800-56A], while L =

KBits in the notation of versions of [SP 800-56B] published prior to the release
of this version of SP 800-56C.)

   c.   *FixedInfo* – a bit string of context-specific data that is appropriate for the relying
key-establishment scheme. As its name suggests, the value of *FixedInfo* does not
change during the execution of the process described below.

        FixedInfo may, for example, include appropriately formatted representations of
the values of *salt* and/or *L*. The inclusion of additional copies of the values of *salt*
and *L* in *FixedInfo* would ensure that each block of derived keying material is
affected by all of the information conveyed in *OtherInput*. See [SP 800-56A] and
[SP 800-56B] for more detailed recommendations concerning the format and
content of *FixedInfo* (also known as *OtherInfo* in earlier versions of those
documents).

Process:

   1.   If $L > 0$, then set $reps = \lceil L / H\_outputBits \rceil$; otherwise, output an error indicator
and exit this process without performing the remaining actions (i.e., omitting steps
2 through 8).

   2.   If $reps > (2^{32} - 1)$, then output an error indicator and exit this process without
performing the remaining actions (i.e., omitting steps 3 through 8).

   3.   Initialize a big-endian 4-byte unsigned integer *counter* as 0x00000000,
corresponding to a 32-bit binary representation of the number zero.

   4.   If *counter* $\|$ *Z* $\|$ *FixedInfo* is more than $max\_H\_inputBits$ bits long, then output an
error indicator and exit this process without performing any of the remaining
actions (i.e., omitting steps 5 through 8).

   5.   Initialize *Result*(0) as an empty bit string (i.e., the null string).

   6.   For $i = 1$ to *reps*, do the following:

        6.1 Increment *counter* by 1.

        6.2 Compute $K(i) = H(counter \| Z \| FixedInfo)$.

        6.3 Set $Result(i) = Result(i - 1) \| K(i)$.

   7.   Set *DerivedKeyingMaterial* equal to the leftmost *L* bits of *Result*(*reps*).

   8.   Output *DerivedKeyingMaterial*.

Output:

       The bit string *DerivedKeyingMaterial* of length *L* bits (or an error indicator).

Notes:

In step 6.2 above, if H(*x*) = *hash*(*x*) or H(*x*) = HMAC-*hash*(*salt*, *x*), the entire output
block of the hash function, *hash*, **shall** be used when computing the output of H. Some

approved choices for *hash* (e.g., SHA-512/224, SHA-512/256, and SHA-384, as specified in [FIPS 180]) include an internal truncation operation. In such a case, the "entire output" of *hash* is the output block as defined in its specification. (For example, in the case of *hash* = SHA-384, the entire output is defined to be a 384-bit block resulting from the internal truncation of a certain 512-bit value).

If H(x) = KMAC#(*salt*, x, *H_outputBits*, *S*), then choosing *H_outputBits* = *L* will likely be the most efficient way to produce the desired *L* bits of keying material.

The derived keying material *DerivedKeyingMaterial* **shall** be computed in its entirety before outputting any portion of it.

4.2 The Auxiliary Function H(x) and Related Parameters

Tables 1, 2, and 3 enumerate the possibilities for the auxiliary function H and provide additional information concerning the values of related parameters such as *H_outputBits* and *max_H_inputBits*. The tables also indicate the range of security strengths that can be supported by each choice for H (see Section 4.1) when used in a key derivation function for a key-establishment scheme specified in SP 800-56A or SP 800-56B.

Table 1: H(x) = *hash*(x) (Option 1)

Hash Function (*hash*)	Byte / Bit Length of Input Blocks	*H_outputBits* (in bits)	*max_H_inputBits* (in bits)	Security Strength *s* supported (in bits)
SHA-1	64 / 512	160	$\leq 2^{64} - 1$	$112 \leq s \leq 160$
SHA-224	64 / 512	224		$112 \leq s \leq 224$
SHA-256	64 / 512	256		$112 \leq s \leq 256$
SHA-512/224	128 / 1024	224	$\leq 2^{128} - 1$	$112 \leq s \leq 224$
SHA-512/256	128 / 1024	256		$112 \leq s \leq 256$
SHA-384	128 / 1024	384		$112 \leq s \leq 384$
SHA-512	128 / 1024	512		$112 \leq s \leq 512$
SHA3-224	144 / 1152	224	Arbitrarily long inputs can be accommodated.	$112 \leq s \leq 224$
SHA3-256	136 / 1088	256		$112 \leq s \leq 256$
SHA3-384	104 / 832	384		$112 \leq s \leq 384$
SHA3-512	72 / 576	512		$112 \leq s \leq 512$

Table 2: H(x) = HMAC-*hash*(*salt*, *x*)   (Option 2)

Hash Function (*hash*)	Effective Byte / Bit Length* of *salt*	*H_outputBits* (in bits)	*max_H_inputBits* (in bits)	Security Strength *s* supported (in bits)
SHA-1	64 / 512	160		$112 \leq s \leq 160$
SHA-224	64 / 512	224	$\leq 2^{64} - 513$	$112 \leq s \leq 224$
SHA-256	64 / 512	256		$112 \leq s \leq 256$
SHA-512/224	128 / 1024	224		$112 \leq s \leq 224$
SHA-512/256	128 / 1024	256	$\leq 2^{128} - 1025$	$112 \leq s \leq 256$
SHA-384	128 / 1024	384		$112 \leq s \leq 384$
SHA-512	128 / 1024	512		$112 \leq s \leq 512$
SHA3-224	144 / 1152	224		$112 \leq s \leq 224$
SHA3-256	136 / 1088	256	Arbitrarily long inputs can be accommodated.	$112 \leq s \leq 256$
SHA3-384	104 / 832	384		$112 \leq s \leq 384$
SHA3-512	72 / 576	512		$112 \leq s \leq 512$

* This Recommendation places no restriction on the length of a chosen *salt* other than the requirement that its byte length be greater than zero, but no greater than the length of a single input block to the hash function, *hash*, used to implement HMAC-*hash*. That freedom of choice is somewhat illusory, however, since the HMAC algorithm will convert an input *salt* value (as needed) into a string of the indicated *hash*-dependent length: A shorter *salt* (used by H as an HMAC key) will be padded, by appending an all-zero bit string, to obtain a string of the indicated length (the length of a single input block for the hash function, *hash*); a longer *salt* will be hashed to produce a shorter string (of bit length *H_outputBits*), which will then be padded (by appending an all-zero bit string) to obtain a string of the indicated length (see [FIPS 198] for additional information).

Table 3: H(x) = KMAC#(*salt*, *x*, *H_outputBits*, "KDF")   (Option 3)

KMAC Variant	Length of a byte-padded *salt* value	Suggested Maximum Byte Length of *salt*	*H_outputBits* (in bits)	*max_H_inputBits* (in bits)	Security Strength *s* supported (in bits)
KMAC128	Multiple of 168 bytes	168 − 4 = 164 **	Choice of 160, 224, 256, 384, 512, or *L*.	Arbitrarily long inputs can be accommodated.	$112 \leq s \leq 128$
KMAC256	Multiple of 136 bytes	136 − 4 = 132 ***			$112 \leq s \leq 256$

** KMAC# prepends a length encoding for the first input data field. For KMAC128, using 164 bytes (or less) of salt leaves room for 4 bytes of prepended length encoding and limits the length of the encoded salt to no more than the length of a single block of input to KMAC128.

*** KMAC# prepends a length encoding for the first input data field. For KMAC256, using 132 bytes (or less) of salt leaves room for 4 bytes of prepended length encoding and limits the length of the encoded salt to no more than the length of a single block of input to KMAC256.

5   Two-Step Key Derivation

This section specifies an **approved** (two-step) extraction-then-expansion key-derivation procedure. Like the one-step key-derivation functions described in Section 4, the input to this two-step procedure includes Z, the shared secret generated during the execution of a key-establishment scheme that is specified in either [SP 800-56A] or [SP 800-56B]); L, a positive integer indicating the desired length (in bits) of the output keying material; and other information (as determined by the particular implementation of the key-establishment scheme and/or key-derivation method). In contrast to the one-step methods, a *salt* value is required to be included as part of the input.

The extraction-then-expansion key-derivation procedure is pictured in Figure 1.

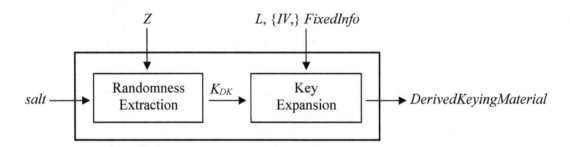

Figure 1: The Extraction-then-Expansion Key-Derivation Procedure

The first (randomness-extraction) step uses either HMAC, as defined in [FIPS 198], or AES-CMAC, as defined in [SP 800-38B]. In either case, there are two inputs: *salt*, which serves as a MAC key, and the shared secret, Z, which serves as the "message." The resulting MAC output is used as a key-derivation key, K_{DK}. The use of this K_{DK} is restricted to a single execution of the key-expansion step of this procedure.

The second (key-expansion) step uses the key-derivation key, K_{DK}, along with the integer L and other appropriate data, as the input to a PRF-based key-derivation function specified in [SP 800-108]. The output returned by that key-derivation function is either secret keying material (in the form of *DerivedKeyingMaterial*, a bit string of length L) or an error indicator.

5.1   Specification of Key-Derivation Procedure

The extraction-then-expansion key-derivation procedure is specified as follows:

Function call: KDM(Z, *OtherInput*).

Options for the Auxiliary MAC Algorithm:

The MAC algorithm employed for randomness extraction **shall** be either an implementation of HMAC as defined in [FIPS 198], based on an **approved** hash function, *hash* (i.e., HMAC-*hash*), or an implementation of AES-CMAC as defined in [SP 800-38B] (i.e., AES-N-CMAC for N = 128, 192, or 256); in either case, the (untruncated) output of the MAC algorithm is used as the key-derivation key for subsequent key expansion. Tables 4 and 5 in Section 5.2 describe the possibilities for the auxiliary MAC algorithm, which **shall** be chosen in accordance with the selection requirements specified in Section 7.

Implementation-Dependent Auxiliary PRF-based KDF:

One of the general-purpose PRF-based key-derivation functions defined in [SP 800-108] **shall** be used for key expansion. These key-derivation functions employ an **approved** MAC algorithm as the PRF. In this Recommendation, the PRF used by the KDF in key expansion is determined by the MAC algorithm that is used for randomness extraction. Specifically:

a. If HMAC-*hash* is used in the randomness-extraction step, then the same HMAC-*hash* (i.e., using the same hash function, *hash*) **shall** be used as the PRF in the key-expansion step; and

b. If either AES-128-CMAC, AES-192-CMAC, or AES-256-CMAC is used in the randomness-extraction step, then only AES-128-CMAC (i.e., the CMAC mode of AES-128) **shall** be used as the PRF in the key-expansion step.

The rationale for these rules is discussed in Section 8.3.

Input:

1. Z – a byte string that represents the shared secret. It is used as the "message" during the execution of the MAC algorithm employed in the randomness-extraction step.

2. *OtherInput*, which includes:

   a. *salt* – a non-null (secret or non-secret) byte string used as the MAC key during the execution of the randomness-extraction step (i.e., step 1 in the process shown below). This *salt* could be, for example, a value computed from nonces exchanged as part of a key-establishment protocol that employs one or more of the key-agreement schemes specified in [SP 800-56A] or [SP 800-56B], a value already shared by the protocol participants, or a value that is pre-determined by the protocol. The possibilities for the length of *salt* are determined by the auxiliary MAC algorithm that is used for randomness extraction:

      (1) The HMAC-*hash* algorithm as defined in [FIPS 198] can accommodate keys of any length up to the maximum bit length permitted for input to the hash function, *hash*; therefore, the length of the byte string *salt* can be as large as allowed for any string used as input to *hash*. However, if the bit length of *salt* is greater than the bit length specified for a single input block for *hash*, then the value of *salt* is replaced by *hash*(*salt*) as part of the HMAC computation. (Input-block lengths for the **approved** hash functions that can be employed to implement HMAC-*hash* are included in column 4 of Table 1 in Section 4.2; also see Table 4 of Section 5.2.) In the absence of an agreed-upon alternative,

the input *salt* value **shall** be an all-zero byte string whose length is equal to that of a single input block for the hash function, *hash*.

(2) AES-*N*-CMAC requires keys that are *N* bits long (for *N* = 128, 192, or 256), depending upon the AES variant that is used in the implementation. The bit length of *salt* **shall** be the bit length required of a key for that AES variant (128 bits for AES-128, 192 bits for AES-192, or 256 bits for AES-256). In the absence of an agreed-upon alternative, the input *salt* value **shall** be an all-zero string of the required bit length.

b. *L* – a positive integer that indicates the length (in bits) of the secret keying material to be derived using the auxiliary PRF-based KDF during the execution of the key-expansion step (i.e., step 2 in the process shown below). The maximum value allowed for *L* is determined by the mode (i.e., Counter Mode, Feedback Mode, or Double-Pipeline Iteration Mode) and implementation details of the chosen KDF, as specified in [SP 800-108]. An error event will occur during the execution of the KDF if *L* is too large.[13]

(Note that *L* = *keydatalen* in the notation of previous versions of [SP 800-56A], while *L* = *KBits* in the notation of versions of [SP 800-56B] published prior to the release of this version of SP 800-56C.)

c. {*IV*} – a bit string included (if required) for use as an initial value during execution of the auxiliary PRF-based KDF; an *IV* **shall** be included in *OtherInput* if and only if the chosen PRF-based KDF is operating in Feedback Mode. It can be either secret or non-secret. It may be an empty string. If the PRF-based KDF is operating in either Counter Mode or Double-Pipeline Iteration Mode, an *IV* **shall not** be included in *OtherInput*. (See [SP 800-108] for details.)

d. *FixedInfo*, including:

(1) *Label* – a bit string that identifies the purpose for the derived keying material. For example, it can be the ASCII encoding of a character string describing the relying application(s) and/or the intended use(s) of the keying material. The value and encoding method used for the *Label* are defined in a larger context, for example, in the protocol that uses this key-derivation procedure. As an alternative to including this string as a separate component of *FixedInfo*, *Label* could be incorporated in *Context* (see below).

(2) *Context* – a bit string of context-specific data appropriate for the relying key-establishment scheme/protocol and the chosen PRF-based KDF.

For recommendations concerning the format and context-specific content of

---

[13] The restrictions on the size of *L* that are given in [SP 800-108] are stated in terms of $n = \lceil L/h \rceil$, where *h* denotes the bit length of an output block of the PRF used to implement the auxiliary KDF. In the case of Counter Mode, the restriction is $n \le 2^r - 1$, where $r \le 32$ is the (implementation-dependent) bit length allocated for the KDF's counter variable. For the other KDF modes, the restriction is simply $n \le 2^{32} - 1$.

Context, see the specifications of *FixedInfo* and/or *OtherInfo* in [SP 800-56A] and/or [SP 800-56B], respectively.

(3) $[L]_2$ – an agreed-upon encoding of L as a bit string that is appropriate for use by the chosen PRF-based KDF (see [SP 800-108] for details). As an alternative to including this string as a separate component of *FixedInfo*, $[L]_2$ could be incorporated in *Context* (see above).

Process:

[Randomness Extraction]

1. Call MAC(*salt, Z, …*) to obtain K_{DK} or an error indicator; if an error occurs, output an error indicator, and exit from this process without performing step 2.

[Key Expansion]

2. Call KDF(K_{DK}, L, {*IV,*} *FixedInfo*) to obtain *DerivedKeyingMaterial* or an error indicator (see [SP 800-108] for details). If an error occurs, output an error indicator; otherwise output *DerivedKeyingMaterial*.

Output:

The bit string *DerivedKeyingMaterial* of length L bits (or an error indicator).

Notes:

When HMAC-*hash* is used as the auxiliary MAC algorithm, the length of K_{DK} is the length of an untruncated output block from the hash function, *hash*. When AES-CMAC is used, then (regardless of the AES variant employed) K_{DK} is a 128-bit binary string. K_{DK} is used (locally) as a key-derivation key by the auxiliary KDF during the key-expansion step, and then **shall be** destroyed (along with all other sensitive locally stored data) after its use. Its value **shall not** be an output of the key-derivation procedure.

[RFC 5869] specifies a version of the above extraction-then-expansion key-derivation procedure using HMAC for both the extraction and expansion steps. For an extensive discussion concerning the rationale for the extract-and-expand mechanisms specified in this Recommendation, see [LNCS 6223].

5.2　The Auxiliary MAC Algorithm and Related Parameters

Tables 4 and 5 enumerate the possibilities for the auxiliary MAC algorithm used for randomness extraction and provide additional information concerning the lengths of the MAC key (i.e., the *salt* value) and the extracted key-derivation key (i.e., K_{DK}). The tables also indicate the range of security strengths that can be supported by each choice for MAC (see Section 5.1) when used for two-step key derivation in a key-establishment scheme specified in SP 800-56A and SP 800-56B.

Table 4: MAC(*salt, Z, ...*) = HMAC-*hash*(*salt, Z*)   (For Randomness Extraction)

Hash Function (*hash*)	Effective Byte / Bit Length* of *salt*	Bit Length of Extracted K_{DK}	Security Strength *s* supported (in bits)
SHA-1	64 / 512	160	$112 \leq s \leq 160$
SHA-224	64 / 512	224	$112 \leq s \leq 224$
SHA-256	64 / 512	256	$112 \leq s \leq 256$
SHA-512/224	128 / 1024	224	$112 \leq s \leq 224$
SHA-512/256	128 / 1024	256	$112 \leq s \leq 256$
SHA-384	128 / 1024	384	$112 \leq s \leq 384$
SHA-512	128 / 1024	512	$112 \leq s \leq 512$
SHA3-224	144 / 1152	224	$112 \leq s \leq 224$
SHA3-256	136 / 1088	256	$112 \leq s \leq 256$
SHA3-384	104 / 832	384	$112 \leq s \leq 384$
SHA3-512	72 / 576	512	$112 \leq s \leq 512$

* This Recommendation places no restriction on the length of a chosen *salt* other than the requirement that its byte length be greater than zero, but no greater than the length of a single input block to the hash function, *hash*, used to implement HMAC-*hash*. That freedom of choice is somewhat illusory, however, since the HMAC algorithm will convert an input *salt* value (as needed) into a string of the indicated *hash*-dependent length: A shorter *salt* (which is used as an HMAC key) will be padded, by appending an all-zero bit string, to obtain a string of the indicated length (the length of a single input block for the hash function, *hash*); a longer *salt* will be hashed to produce a shorter string, which will then be padded (by appending an all-zero bit string) to obtain a string of the indicated length. (See [FIPS 198] for additional information.)

Note: The hash function, *hash*, used by the HMAC algorithm employed during randomness extraction **shall** be used again in the subsequent key-expansion step to implement the HMAC algorithm that is employed as a PRF by the auxiliary PRF-based KDF.

Table 5: MAC(*salt, Z,* ...) = AES-*N*-CMAC(*salt, Z*) (For Randomness Extraction)

AES Variant used by AES-CMAC	Bit Length of *salt* for AES-CMAC	Bit Length of Extracted K_{DK}	Security Strength *s* supported (in bits)
AES-128	128		
AES-192	192	128	$112 \leq s \leq 128$
AES-256	256		

Note: Regardless of which AES variant is used by the AES-CMAC algorithm during randomness-extraction, the 128-bit AES block size determines the bit length of the resulting K_{DK}. To accommodate the use of this 128-bit K_{DK} as a key-derivation key, the CMAC mode of AES-128 **shall** be the PRF employed by the auxiliary PRF-based KDF in the subsequent key-expansion step.

6   Application-Specific Key-Derivation Methods

Additional **approved** application-specific key-derivation methods are enumerated in [SP 800-135]. Unless an explicit exception is made in [SP 800-135], any hash function or MAC algorithm employed by the key-derivation methods enumerated in [SP 800-135] **shall** be **approved** and **shall** also meet the selection requirements specified in this Recommendation (i.e., SP 800-56C).

7   Selecting Hash Functions and MAC Algorithms

The key-derivation methods specified in this Recommendation, as well as those enumerated in [SP 800-135], use hash functions and/or message authentication code (MAC) algorithms as auxiliary functions. In particular:

- The one-step key-derivation functions that are specified in Section 4.1 of this Recommendation employ an appropriate choice of hash function (*hash*), an HMAC algorithm based on an appropriate choice of hash function (HMAC-*hash*), or one of two KMAC variants (KMAC128 or KMAC256) to implement the auxiliary function H.

- The extraction-then-expansion key-derivation procedure specified in Section 5.1 employs either an HMAC algorithm based on an appropriate choice of hash function (HMAC-*hash*) for both randomness extraction and key expansion, or an appropriate variant of the AES-CMAC algorithm (i.e., AES-N-CMAC for $N = 128$, 192, or 256) for randomness extraction together with AES-128-CMAC for key expansion.

Unless explicitly stated to the contrary, (e.g., in [SP 800-135]), the following requirements apply to the hash functions and MAC algorithms employed for key derivation:

- Whenever a hash function is employed (including as the primitive used by HMAC), an **approved** hash function **shall** be used. [FIPS 180] and [FIPS 202] specify **approved** hash functions.

- Whenever an HMAC algorithm is employed, the HMAC implementation **shall** conform to the specifications found in [FIPS 198].

- Whenever a KMAC variant (KMAC128 or KMAC256) is employed, the KMAC implementation **shall** conform to the specifications found in [SP 800-185].

- Whenever an AES-CMAC algorithm is employed, the implementation of AES **shall** conform to [FIPS 197] and the AES-CMAC implementation **shall** conform to [SP 800-38B].

As specified in [SP 800-56A] and [SP 800-56B], an **approved** key-establishment scheme can be implemented with parameters of various types and sizes that will impact the estimated maximum security strength that can be supported by the resulting scheme. When a key-establishment scheme employs a choice of parameters that are associated with a targeted security strength of s bits, the selection of a hash function, HMAC, KMAC, or AES-CMAC employed during the implementation of its key-derivation method **shall** conform to the following restrictions:

- An **approved** hash function **shall** be employed (whether alone or as the primitive used by HMAC) in the implementation of a one-step or two-step key-derivation method only if its output block length (in bits) is greater than or equal to s.

- For the purposes of implementing one-step key derivation only: KMAC128 **shall** be employed only in instances where s is 128 bits or less; KMAC256 **shall** be employed only in instances where s is 256 bits or less. (See, however, the note below.)

- For the purposes of implementing two-step key derivation only: AES-CMAC **shall** be employed only in instances where s is 128 bits or less. (See the note following Table 5.)

Tables 1 through 5 (in Sections 4.1 and 5.1) can be consulted to determine which hash functions and/or MAC algorithms are **approved** for use when a key-derivation method specified in this Recommendation is used by an **approved** key-establishment scheme to support a targeted security strength of s bits.

Note: At the time of publication of this Recommendation, a key-establishment scheme implemented in accordance with either [SP 800-56A] or [SP 800-56B] can have a targeted security strength of at most 256 bits.

<h1>8   Further Discussion</h1>

In this section, the following issues are discussed:

8.1   Using a Truncated Hash Function

SHA-224, SHA-512/224, SHA-512/256 and SHA-384 are among the **approved** hash functions specified in [FIPS 180]. SHA-224 is a truncated version of SHA-256, while SHA-512/224, SHA-512/256, and SHA-384 are truncated versions of SHA-512. (Each of these truncated versions uses a specific initial chaining value, which is different from the initial chaining value used by the untruncated version.) In applications that require a relatively long bit string of derived keying material, implementing the key-derivation methods specified in this Recommendation with a truncated version of a hash function may be less efficient than using the corresponding untruncated version (i.e., SHA-256 or SHA-512).

8.2   The Choice of a Salt Value

In this Recommendation, the MAC algorithms employed either in a one-step key-derivation method or in the randomness-extraction step of a two-step key derivation method use a salt value as a MAC key (see Sections 4 and 5). This Recommendation does not require the use of a randomly selected salt value. In particular, if there is no means to select a salt value and share it with all of the participants during a key-establishment transaction, then this Recommendation specifies that a predetermined default (e.g., all-zero) byte string be used as the salt value. The benefits of using "random" salt values, when possible, are discussed (briefly) in Section 3.1 ("To salt or not to salt.") of [RFC 5869], and in greater detail in [LNCS 6223].

8.3   MAC Algorithms used for Extraction and Expansion

Provided that the targeted security strength can be supported (see Tables 4 and 5 in Section 5.2), this Recommendation permits either HMAC-*hash* (i.e., HMAC implemented with an appropriately chosen **approved** hash function, *hash*) or AES-CMAC (i.e., the CMAC mode of AES-128, AES-192, or AES-256) to be selected as the MAC algorithm used in the randomness-extraction step of the key-derivation procedure specified in Section 5.1.

The PRF-based KDF used in the key-expansion step of the procedure also requires an appropriate MAC (to serve as the PRF). While it may be technically feasible (in some cases) to employ completely different MAC algorithms in the two steps of the specified key-derivation procedure, this Recommendation does not permit such flexibility. Instead, the following restrictions have been placed on MAC selection (see Sections 5 and 7):

- When HMAC-*hash* is chosen for use in the randomness-extraction step, the same MAC algorithm (i.e., HMAC-*hash* with the same **approved** hash function, *hash*) **shall** be employed to implement the PRF-based KDF used in the key-expansion step.

- When AES-128-CMAC, AES-192-CMAC, or AES-256-CMAC is chosen for use in the randomness-extraction step, the MAC algorithm employed by the PRF-based KDF used in the key-expansion step **shall** be AES-128-CMAC, the CMAC mode of AES-128. (AES-128 is the only AES variant that can employ the 128-bit K_{DK} produced by AES-N-CMAC during the randomness-extraction step.)

- The MAC algorithm selected for the implementation of a two-step key-derivation method **shall** be capable of supporting the targeted security strength, as determined by consulting Tables 4 and 5 in Section 5.2. (This limits the use of AES-CMAC to cases where the targeted security strength is no more than 128 bits.)

The imposed restrictions are intended to reduce the overall complexity of the resulting implementations, promote interoperability, and simplify the negotiation of the parameters and auxiliary functions affecting the security strength supported by the key-derivation procedure.

Note: At this time, KMAC has not been specified for use in the implementation of a two-step key derivation procedure. This restriction may be reconsidered once a KMAC-based KDF has been **approved** for use as a PRF-based KDF in a revision of [SP 800-108].

8.4 Destruction of Sensitive Locally Stored Data

Good security practice dictates that implementations of key-derivation methods include steps that destroy potentially sensitive locally stored data that is created (and/or copied for use) during the execution of a particular process; there is no need to retain such data after the process has been completed. Examples of potentially sensitive locally stored data include local copies of shared secrets that are employed during the execution of a particular process, intermediate results produced during computations, and locally stored duplicates of values that are ultimately output by the process. The destruction of such locally stored data ideally occurs prior to or during any exit from the process. This is intended to limit opportunities for unauthorized access to sensitive information that might compromise a key-establishment transaction.

It is not possible to anticipate the form of all possible implementations of the key-derivation methods specified in this Recommendation, making it impossible to enumerate all potentially sensitive data that might be locally stored by a process employed in a particular implementation. Nevertheless, the destruction of any potentially sensitive locally stored data is an obligation of all implementations.

Appendix A—References

[SP 800-38B]   NIST Special Publication (SP) 800-38B, *Recommendation for Block Cipher Modes of Operation – The CMAC Mode for Authentication*, May 2005.
                    https://doi.org/10.6028/NIST.SP.800-38B

[SP 800-56A]   NIST Special Publication (SP) 800-56A Revision 3, *Recommendation for Pair-Wise Key-Establishment Schemes Using Discrete Logarithm Cryptography*, April 2018.
                    https://doi.org/10.6028/NIST.SP.800-56Ar3

[SP 800-56B]   NIST Special Publication (SP) 800-56B Revision 1, *Recommendation for Pair-Wise Key-Establishment Schemes Using Integer Factorization Cryptography*, September 2014.
                    https://doi.org/10.6028/NIST.SP.800-56Br1

[SP 800-57]   NIST Special Publication (SP) 800-57 Part 1 Revision 4, *Recommendation for Key Management Part 1: General*, January 2016.
                    https://doi.org/10.6028/NIST.SP.800-57pt1r4

[SP 800-108]   NIST Special Publication (SP) 800-108, *Recommendation for Key Derivation Using Pseudorandom Functions*, October 2009.
                    https://doi.org/10.6028/NIST.SP.800-108

[SP 800-131A]   NIST Special Publication (SP) 800-131A Revision 1, *Transitions: Recommendation for Transitioning the Use of Cryptographic Algorithms and Key Lengths*, November 2015.
                    https://doi.org/10.6028/NIST.SP.800-131Ar1

[SP 800-135]   NIST Special Publication (SP) 800-135 Revision 1, *Recommendation for Existing Application-Specific Key Derivation Functions*, December 2011.
                    https://doi.org/10.6028/NIST.SP.800-135r1

[SP 800-185]   NIST Special Publication (SP) 800-185, *SHA-3 Derived Functions: cSHAKE, KMAC, TupleHash and ParallelHash*, December 2016.
                    https://doi.org/10.6028/NIST.SP.800-185

[FIPS 180]   Federal Information Processing Standard (FIPS) 180-4, *Secure Hash Standard*, August 2015.
                    https://doi.org/10.6028/NIST.FIPS.180-4

[FIPS 197]   Federal Information Processing Standard (FIPS) 197, *Advanced Encryption Standard*, November 2001.
                    https://doi.org/10.6028/NIST.FIPS.197

[FIPS 198]   Federal Information Processing Standard (FIPS) 198-1, *The Keyed-Hash Message Authentication Code (HMAC)*, July 2008.
https://doi.org/10.6028/NIST.FIPS.198-1

[FIPS 202]   Federal Information Processing Standard (FIPS) 202, *SHA-3 Standard: Permutation-Based Hash and Extendable-Output Functions*, August 2015.
https://doi.org/10.6028/NIST.FIPS.202

[RFC 5869]   IETF Request for Comments (RFC) 5869, HMAC-based Extract-and-Expand Key Derivation Function (HKDF), May 2010.
https://doi.org/10.17487/RFC5869

[LNCS 6223]   H. Krawczyk. "Cryptographic Extraction and Key Derivation: The HKDF Scheme," in *Advances in Cryptology - Crypto'2010*, Lecture Notes in Computer Science Vol. 6223, pp. 631-648. Springer. 2010.
https://doi.org/10.1007/978-3-642-14623-7_34

Appendix B—Revisions (Informative)

The original SP 800-56C (published in November 2011) focused entirely on the specification of a two-step extraction-then-expansion key-derivation procedure to be used in conjunction with a key-establishment scheme from either [SP 800-56A] or [SP 800-56B]; it provided an alternative to the one-step key-derivation functions that were already included in those companion publications.

The 2018 revision of SP 800-56C reorganizes the original content (it still includes the specification of an extraction-then-expansion key-derivation procedure) to also include the specification of a family of one-step key-derivation functions, expanding on material that was previously found only in SP 800-56A and SP 800-56B. This change was made in support of the removal of detailed descriptions of key-derivation methods from SP 800-56A and a future revision of SP 800-56B. The consolidation of specifications in SP 800-56C revision 1 will promote consistency between the key-derivation options available for use with an **approved** key-establishment scheme chosen from either of those companion NIST publications. (There will, however, continue to be a number of application-specific key-derivation methods specified in [SP 800-135].)

Specifically named key-establishment "parameter sets" (FA – FC for finite-field cryptography (FFC); EA – EE for elliptic-curve cryptography (ECC); and IA – IB for integer-factorization cryptography (IFC)) are no longer used as guides for choosing the auxiliary functions employed by a key-derivation method. Instead, SP 800-56C revision 1 indicates the security strengths that can be supported by the various possibilities for the auxiliary functions. Implementers are expected to let the targeted security strength of the key-establishment scheme guide their choices. Of course, each of the named parameter sets was associated with a targeted security strength, so this is more a change of perspective than of substance. The change is, however, consistent with the revision of [SP 800-56A], which de-emphasizes (in the FFC case) or eliminates (in the ECC case) the use of named parameter (size) sets.

There is one substantial change to the specification of key-derivation methods that is worth noting: a KMAC-based option for implementing the auxiliary function H has been added to the specification of one-step key-derivation functions (see Section 4.1). At this time, however, KMAC has not been specified for use as an auxiliary MAC algorithm in the two-step extraction-then-expansion key-derivation procedure (see Section 8.3).

Given the extent to which SP 800-56C has been revised, it is impractical to list all of the changes that have been made to the original text. It is recommended that SP 800-56C revision 1 be read in its entirety in order to gain familiarity with the details of the current specifications for both one-step and two-step key-derivation methods used in **approved** key-establishment schemes.